Diabetic Fish and Seafood Cookbook

50 Easy and Healthy Diabetic Recipes for the Newly Diagnosed to Manage Prediabetes and Type 2 Diabetes

Melissa Mitchell

Table of Contents

Introduction

Diabetes Mellitus ("diabetes" for short) is a severe disease that occurs when your body has difficulty properly regulating the amount of dissolved sugar (glucose) in your bloodstream. It is unrelated to a similarly named disorder, "Diabetes Insipidus", which involves kidney-related fluid retention problems.

To understand diabetes, it is necessary first to understand the role glucose plays in the body and what can happen when glucose regulation fails. Blood sugar levels become dangerously low or high.

The tissues and cells that make up the human body are living things and require food to stay alive. The food cells eat a type of sugar called glucose. Fixed in place as they are, the body's cells are entirely dependent on the bloodstream in which they are bathed to bring glucose to them. Without access to adequate glucose, the body's cells have nothing to fuel themselves with and soon die.

Human beings eat food, not glucose. Human foods get converted into glucose as a part of the normal digestion process. Once converted, glucose enters the bloodstream, causing dissolved glucose inside the blood to rise. The bloodstream then carries the dissolved glucose to the various tissues and cells of the body.

Though glucose may be available in the blood, nearby cells cannot access that glucose without the aid of a chemical hormone called insulin. Insulin acts as a key to open the cells, allowing them to receive and utilize available glucose. Cells absorb glucose from the blood in the presence of insulin, and blood sugar levels drop as sugar leaves the blood and enters the cells. Insulin can be thought of as a bridge for glucose between the bloodstream and cells.

The body is designed to regulate and buffer the amount of glucose dissolved in the blood to maintain a steady supply to meet cell needs. The pancreas, one of your body's many organs, produces, stores, and releases insulin into the bloodstream to bring glucose levels back down.

The concentration of glucose available in the bloodstream at any given moment is dependent on the amount and type of foods that people eat. Refined carbohydrates, candy, and sweets are easy to break down into glucose. Correspondingly, blood glucose levels rise rapidly after such foods have been eaten. In contrast, blood sugars rise gradually and slowly after eating more complex, unrefined carbohydrates (oatmeal, apples, baked potatoes, etc.), which require more digestive steps to take place before glucose can be yielded. Faced with rapidly rising blood glucose concentrations, the body must react quickly by releasing large amounts of insulin at once or risk a dangerous condition called Hyperglycemia (high blood sugar) which will be described below.

The influx of insulin enables cells to utilize glucose, and glucose concentrations drop. While glucose levels can rise and fall rapidly, insulin levels change much more slowly. When a large amount of simple sugar is eaten, the bloodstream quickly becomes flooded with glucose. The pancreas releases insulin in response to the increased sugar. The glucose rapidly enters the cells, but the high insulin levels remain in the bloodstream for some time.

This can result in an overabundance of insulin in the blood, which can trigger feelings of hunger and even hypoglycemia (low blood sugar), another serious condition. When blood glucose concentrations rise more gradually, there is less need for dramatic compensation. Insulin can be released in a more controlled and safer manner, requiring the body to experience less strain. This more gradual process will leave you feeling "full" or content for a more extended period.

For these reasons, it is best for overall health to limit the amount and frequency of sweets and refined sugars in your diet. Instead, eat more complex sugars such as raw fruit, whole wheat bread and pasta, and beans. The difference between simple and complex sugars (carbohydrates) is exemplified by the difference between white (simple) and whole wheat (more difficult) bread.

Insulin is the critical key to the cell's ability to use glucose. Problems with insulin production or how insulin is recognized by the cells can easily cause the body's carefully balanced glucose metabolism system to get out of control. When either of these problems occurs, diabetes develops, blood sugar levels surge and crash, and the body risks becoming damaged.

Diabetes: Definition, Causes, And Symptoms

What Is Diabetes?

Diabetes is a disease that affects your body's ability to produce or use insulin. Insulin is a hormone. When your body turns the food you eat into energy (also called sugar or glucose), insulin is released to help transport this energy to the cells. Insulin acts as a "key." Its chemical message tells the cell to open and receive glucose. If you produce little or no insulin or are insulin resistant, too much sugar remains in your blood. Blood glucose levels are higher than average for individuals with diabetes. There are two main types of diabetes: Type 1 and Type 2.

Diabetes is a disease that occurs when your blood glucose, also called blood sugar, is too high. Blood glucose is your primary source of energy and comes from the food you eat. Insulin, a hormone made by the pancreas, helps glucose from food get into your cells to be used for energy. Sometimes your body doesn't make enough or any insulin or doesn't use insulin well. Glucose then stays in your blood and doesn't reach your cells.

What Is Type 1 Diabetes?

When you are affected with Type 1 diabetes, your pancreas does not produce insulin. Type 1 diabetes, once called juvenile diabetes, is often diagnosed in children or teens. However, it can also occur in adults. This type accounts for 5-10 percent of people with diabetes.

What Is Type 2 Diabetes?

Type 2 diabetes occurs when the body does not produce enough insulin or when the cells cannot use insulin properly, which is called insulin resistance. Type 2 diabetes is commonly called "adult-onset diabetes" since it is diagnosed later in life, generally after 45. It accounts for 90-95 percent of people with diabetes. In recent years, Type 2 diabetes has been diagnosed in younger people, including children, more frequently than in the past.

Gestational Diabetes

Gestational diabetes develops in some women when they are pregnant. Most of the time, this type of diabetes goes away after the baby is born. However, if you've had gestational diabetes, you have a greater chance of developing type 2 diabetes later in life. Sometimes diabetes diagnosed during pregnancy is type 2 diabetes.

Who Gets Diabetes? What Are The Risk Factors?

Factors that increase your risk differ depending on the type of diabetes you ultimately develop.

Risk Factors For Type 1 Diabetes Include:

- We are having a family history (parent or sibling) of type 1 diabetes.
- Injury to the pancreas (such as by infection, tumor, surgery, or accident).
- Presence of autoantibodies (antibodies that mistakenly attack your own body's tissues or organs).
- Physical stress (such as surgery or illness).
- Exposure to illnesses caused by viruses.

Risk Factors For Prediabetes And Type 2 Diabetes Include:

- Family history (parent or sibling) of prediabetes or type 2 diabetes.
- I am African-American, Hispanic, Native American, Asian-American race, or Pacific Islander.
- It is overweight.
- I had high blood pressure.
- I am having low HDL cholesterol (the "good" cholesterol) and a high triglyceride level.
- She was physically inactive.
- They were being aged 45 or older.

- I am having gestational diabetes or giving birth to a baby weighing more than 9 pounds.
- I have polycystic ovary syndrome.
- I was having a history of heart disease or stroke.
- She is a smoker.

Risk Factors For Gestational Diabetes Include:

- Family history (parent or sibling) of prediabetes or type 2 diabetes.
- Being African-American, Hispanic, Native American, or Asian-American.
- You are overweight before your pregnancy.
- They are over 25 years of age.

Symptoms And Causes

What Causes Diabetes?

The cause of diabetes, regardless of the type, is having too much glucose circulating in your bloodstream. However, the reason why your blood glucose levels are high differs depending on the type of diabetes.

1. Causes Of Type 1 Diabetes: This is an immune system disease. Your body attacks and destroys insulin-producing cells in your pancreas. Without insulin to allow glucose to enter your cells, glucose builds up in your bloodstream. Genes may also play a role in some patients. Also, a virus may trigger an immune system attack.

2. Cause Of Type 2 Diabetes And Prediabetes: Your body's cells don't allow insulin to work as it should to let glucose into its cells. Your body's cells have become resistant to insulin. Your pancreas can't keep up and make enough insulin to overcome this resistance. Glucose levels rise in your bloodstream.

3. Gestational Diabetes: Hormones produced by the placenta during pregnancy make your body's cells more resistant to insulin. Your pancreas can't make enough insulin to overcome this resistance. Too much glucose remains in your bloodstream.

What Causes Diabetes?

Genetics, lifestyle, and environment can be causes of diabetes. Eating an unhealthy diet, being overweight or obese, and not exercising enough may play a role in developing diabetes, particularly Type 2 diabetes. An autoimmune response causes type 1 diabetes. The body's immune system attacks and destroys the insulin-producing beta cells in the pancreas.

How Does Diabetes Affect My Body?

Over time, high blood sugar levels (also called hyperglycemia) can lead to kidney disease, heart disease, and blindness. The excess sugar in the bloodstream can damage the tiny blood vessels in your eyes and kidneys and can harden or narrow your arteries.

What Are The Symptoms Of Diabetes?

- Extreme thirst
- Frequent urination
- Blurry vision
- Extreme hunger
- Increased tiredness
- Unusual weight loss

What Health Problems Can People With Diabetes Develop?

Over time, high blood glucose leads to problems such as:

- Heart disease
- Stroke
- Kidney disease
- Eye problems
- Dental disease
- Nerve damage
- Foot problems

You can take steps to lower your chances of developing these diabetes-related health problems.

How Can I Find Out If I Have Diabetes?

Sometimes a routine exam by an eye doctor or foot doctor will reveal diabetes. Diabetes affects the circulation to your feet and the tiny blood vessels in your eyes. If your eye doctor or your foot doctor suspects you have diabetes, they will recommend seeing your regular physician for a blood sugar level test. The most common test is a fasting blood glucose test. After not eating for at least eight hours, your doctor will usually take a blood sample overnight. The standard, non-diabetic range for fasting blood glucose is 70 to 110 mg/dl. If your level is 126 mg/dl or greater, you may have diabetes.

How Is Diabetes Managed?

Diabetes affects your whole body. To best manage diabetes, you'll need to take steps to keep your risk factors under control and within the normal range, including:

- Keep your blood glucose levels as near to normal as possible by following a diet plan, taking prescribed medication, and increasing your activity level.
- Maintain your blood cholesterol (HDL and LDL levels) and triglyceride levels near the normal ranges as possible.
- Control your blood pressure. Your blood pressure should not be over 140/90 mmHg.

You hold the keys to managing your diabetes by:

We are planning what you eat and following a healthy meal plan. Follow a Mediterranean diet (vegetables, whole grains, beans, fruits, healthy fats, low sugar) or Dash diet. These diets are high in nutrition and fiber and low in fats and calories. See a registered dietitian for help understanding nutrition and meal planning.

- I am exercising regularly. Try to exercise for at least 30 minutes most days of the week. Walk, swim or find some activity you enjoy.
- You are losing weight if you are overweight. Work with your healthcare team to develop a weight-loss plan.
- Taking medication and insulin, if prescribed, and closely following recommendations on how and when to take it.
- We are monitoring your blood glucose and blood pressure levels at home.
- You are keeping your appointments with your healthcare providers and having laboratory tests completed as ordered by your doctor.
- I am quitting smoking (if you smoke).
- You have a lot of control – on a day-to-day basis – in

DIABETIC FISH AND SEAFOOD RECIPES

1. Char-Grilled Fish Kebabs With Pesto Potatoes

Total Time: 50-60 mins

Ingredients

- Kebabs
- 7 oz Mackerel fillet

- 7 oz Kingfish fillet
- 7 oz Salmon fillet
- 7 oz Ling fillet
- 12 Shallots
- ¼ cup Olive oil
- 1.5 tbsp Red Wine Vinegar
- 1 clove Garlic, crushed
- Pinch Salt & Black Pepper
- Salad
- 21 oz baby Carisma Potatoes, quartered
- 6 cups baby spinach leaves
- 6 cups Broccolini
- 375g mini Roma Tomatoes or Cherry Tomatoes, halved
- 3 tbsp Basil Pesto

Sides

- 3 small Corn Cobs cut in half or 6 small frozen Corn Cobs

Method

- Preheat the oven to 200o or 180oC fan-forced. Place potato quarters on the oven tray and toss in the olive oil. Season with salt, pepper, and roast in the oven for 40-45 minutes or until tender and golden. Please note-cooking times may vary slightly depending on your oven.
- Cut mackerel, kingfish, salmon, and ling each into 12 equal-sized cubes and place them in a large shallow bowl.

- Make garlic marinade: whisk olive oil, red wine vinegar, and garlic together. Pour over fish and toss well to combine. Cover with plastic wrap and set aside for 30 minutes.
- Meanwhile, bring a steamer saucepan of water to a boil. Add corn and broccolini to the steamer and cook until just soft.
- Transfer cooked potatoes to a bowl, add the baby spinach, broccoli, and halved tomatoes. Add the pesto and toss to coat well.
- Cut green onions into 4 cm lengths. On the bamboo skewer, place a piece of green onion, then thread on one piece of each fish, finishing with a piece of green onion. Repeat with remaining fish and green onion to make 12 skewers.
- Heat a barbecue or char-grill plate to cook kebabs for about a minute on each of 4 sides or until fish is opaque.
- Serve 2 fish kebabs with pesto potato salad and corncob.

Nutrition

- Carbohydrate: 28.5g| Total Fat: 25g| Saturated Fat: 4.11g| Dietary fibre: 16.3g| Sodium: 366mg

2. Grilled Salmon

Prep Time: 1 hr

Cook Time: 12 mins

Ingredients

- 4 6 oz Salmon Fillets
- 1 garlic clove minced

- 1 teaspoon smoked paprika
- 1/4 teaspoon cayenne pepper
- 2 tablespoons parsley chopped fine
- 2 tablespoon thyme
- 1 tablespoon rosemary
- The juice of 1 lemon
- 1/2 cup extra virgin olive oil
- 2 tablespoons soy sauce

Instructions

- Rinse salmon fillets and pat dry.
- Arrange the fillets' skin side down on a baking dish.
- Rub each fillet with herb and spice mixture, making sure to coat each fillet well.
- Combine olive oil, soy sauce, and the juice of one lemon in a bowl.
- Whisk together and pour over the fillets.
- Seal and chill. Marinate for 30-45 minutes.
- Heat grill pan or outdoor grill until piping hot.
- Brush grill grates with olive oil to prevent the fish from sticking.
- Remove fish from the marinade and place it on a very hot grill.
- When the salmon starts to lighten in color, about 6 minutes use a spatula to flip it over on the grill.

- Cook for another 6 minutes or until fish flakes easily with a fork.
- Remove with spatula, garnish with lemon.
- Enjoy.

Nutritional Value

Carbohydrates: 9g | Protein: 12g | Fat: 22g | Cholesterol: 104mg | Sodium: 366mg | Potassium: 331mg | Fiber: 1g | Calcium: 60mg

3. Easy Low Carb Baked Fish

Prep Time: 5 minutes

Cook Time: 25 minutes

Total Time: 30 minutes

Ingredients

- 3 oz Fish fillets- 1 per person

- ¼ tsp Seafood seasoning of choice I use Old Bay Low Sodium Seasoning
- Paprika
- Salt and pepper
- Lemon quarters

Instructions

- Preheat oven to 375 degrees.
- Line a baking pan with parchment paper or foil.
- Place fillets on pan and season liberally with seafood seasoning, paprika, salt, and pepper.
- Bake for 25 minutes or until fish flakes easily.
- Serve with lemon quarters.

Nutrition Facts

- Sodium: 44mg| Potassium: 256mg| Protein: 17g| Iron: 0.5mg

4. Salmon & Shrimp Pasta

Prep Time: 5 minutes

Cook Time: 20 minutes

Total Time: 25 minutes

Ingredients

- 2½ oz. salmon
- 2½ oz. shrimp
- 1½ oz. whole wheat pasta
- 2 tbsp. light sour cream
- ¼ tsp. curry powder
- ¼ tsp. paprika
- ¼ tsp. black pepper
- Chives (optional)

Instructions

- Cook the salmon in the oven at 400 F (200 C) for about 15 min. (depending on how large the piece is). Remove the skin and any brown fat after cooking.
- Cook the pasta according to the instructions on the package. You want the pasta to be done around the same time as the salmon, so based on how long the pasta needs to boil, wait until the salmon only has that long left to cook before placing the pasta in the boiling water.

- Cook the shrimp for 2-3 minutes in lightly salted water until they just start turning pink. You also want the shrimp to finish cooking around the same time as the salmon and pasta, so wait until those ingredients only have a few minutes left before cooking your shrimp. Alternatively, you could buy your shrimp pre-cooked, in which case you'll just skip this step.
- Flake the salmon into small pieces.
- Add the pasta, flaked salmon, and shrimp to a bowl and mix.
- In a small bowl, mix the sour cream and spices until combined. Drizzle over the pasta.
- Garnish with chives to taste.

Nutrition Facts

- Fat: 10.1g| Saturated Fat: 2g| Polyunsaturated Fat: 0.1g| Monounsaturated Fat: 0.2g| Cholesterol: 154.7mg| Sodium: 330.9mg| Potassium: 44.3mg| Carbohydrates: 32.1g| Fiber: 5.2g| Sugar: 1.6g| Protein: 39g

5. Seafood Sausage Gumbo

Prep Time:10 minutes

Cook Time:55 minutes

Total Time:1 hour 5 minutes

Ingredients

- 12 ounces spicy chicken or turkey sausage links (cut into 1-inch slices)
- 2 tablespoons olive oil (extra virgin)
- 1 cup onions (diced)
- ½ cup red bell pepper (chopped)
- ½ cup green bell pepper (chopped)
- 2 cloves garlic (finely minced)
- 2½ cups chicken broth or stock
- 1½ cups crushed tomatoes (no-salt-added)
- ½ teaspoon ground cumin
- ¼ teaspoon cayenne pepper
- ¼ teaspoon kosher salt
- ¼ teaspoon freshly ground black pepper
- 1 bay leaf
- ¾ pound shrimp (peeled and deveined)
- ½ pound scallops
- 6 ounces lump crabmeat
- 1 tablespoon fresh parsley (chopped)

Instructions

- In a large stockpot or Dutch oven, sauté the sausage over medium heat until it starts to brown. Precooked sausage will take about 5 minutes, the un-cooked sausage will take about 15 minutes.

- Transfer the browned sausage to a plate lined with paper towels.
- In the same pot, add the oil along with the onions, bell peppers, and garlic. Stir to combine, then cook for about 10 minutes or until the onions start to become translucent.
- Add the chicken broth, tomatoes, cumin, cayenne, salt, pepper, and bay leaf to the pot.
- Increase the heat to medium-high and bring to a boil, then reduce the heat and simmer, uncovered, for about 30 minutes.
- Add the shrimp and scallops to the pot and simmer for about 5 minutes.
- Add the crab and sausage, then simmer for another 5 minutes or until everything is heated through.
- Ladle into 6 bowls and garnish with fresh parsley.

Nutrition Facts

- Fat: 12.6g| Saturated Fat: 2.2g| Polyunsaturated Fat: 2.4g| Monounsaturated Fat: 1.7g| Cholesterol: 94.6mg| Sodium: 672.5mg| Potassium: 560.6mg| Carbohydrates: 16.2g| Fiber: 2.6g| Sugar: 4.3g| Protein: 28.5g

6. Cumin-Crusted Fish Fillets

Total Time: 15 Minutes

Ingredients

- 1/2 to 1 Tbsp ground cumin
- 1/4 tsp thyme
- 1 tsp paprika
- 1/2 tsp lemon pepper
- 1 lb white fish fillets (like walleye, halibut, or cod)
- 1/2 Tbsp canola oil
- 2 Tbsp chopped parsley
- Lemon or lime wedges

Directions

- In a small bowl, mix cumin, thyme, paprika, and lemon pepper.
- Rub spice mixture on both sides of fillets.
- In a large skillet, set over medium heat, heat canola oil. Add fish fillets and cook until browned on both sides and fish is opaque in the center about 4 minutes per side.
- Sprinkle with parsley and serve immediately with lemon or lime wedges.

Nutritional Information

- Fat: 3.5g| Fiber: 1g| Sodium: 100mg| Cholesterol: 100mg| Protein: 22g| Carbohydrates: 1g

7. Salmon With Cilantro-Lime Salsa

Preparation Time: 10 To 15 Minutes

Cooking Time: 10 To 15 Minute

Ingredients

- Salmon
- 6-8 ounces skin-on salmon (2 fillets)
- 1/4 teaspoon each kosher salt and pepper (mixed)
- 1/2 teaspoon each chili powder, garlic powder, and paprika (mixed)
- 1 tablespoon of olive oil

- Cilantro-Lime Salsa
- 1 tablespoon of chopped cilantro
- 1/2 teaspoon of lime juice
- 1/2 teaspoon garlic clove
- 1/4 cup of quartered cherry tomatoes
- 1 tablespoon of diced red onion
- 1/2 tablespoon of olive oil
- Salt and pepper to taste

Directions

- Combine the first six ingredients for Cilantro-Lime Salsa in a bowl. Add salt and pepper mixture to taste. Set aside or place in the refrigerator until ready to use.
- Pat the salmon skin dry with a paper towel. This step is necessary for nice, crispy skin. Season the skin with half of your salt and pepper mix.
- Season the flesh side of the salmon with the salt and pepper mix and the chili powder, garlic powder, and paprika mix.
- Heat 1 tablespoon of olive oil in a skillet over medium-high heat.
- Once the oil is shimmering, place the salmon skin-side down; hold down for 10 to 15 seconds until it relaxes and lies flat.
- Cook for about 5 minutes over medium-high heat before flipping over. If you feel resistance as you try to flip the

salmon, let it cook a couple of minutes longer. Tip: You should be able to slide the spatula relatively easily under the fish when getting ready to flip it.

- Turn down the heat, flip to the flesh side and let it cook over medium heat for about 3 to 5 minutes, until golden brown. Depending on the thickness of the salmon, you may want to cook it a little longer or less.
- The fish should be opaque (pink) when done. Test for doneness by slightly cutting open the thickest part of the salmon. If it flakes, you're done!
- Serve the salmon topped with the Cilantro-Lime Salsa and your choice of side.

Nutrition Information

- Carbohydrates: 4g, Protein: 18g, Fat: 14g, Cholesterol: 634mg, Sodium: 289mg, Fiber: 1g

8. Tarragon Seafood Pasta Salad

Preparation Time: 35 Minutes

Ingredients

- Water
- 2 tablespoons curry powder
- 8 ounces uncooked penne (tubular pasta)
- 3/4 pound medium shrimp, cooked and peeled (fully-cooked thawed frozen shrimp work well)
- 4 ounces smoked salmon, diced
- 1 1/2 cups lightly steamed, coarsely chopped asparagus
- 1 tablespoon chopped fresh tarragon (or 1 teaspoon dry)
- 1 teaspoon fresh-squeezed lemon juice
- 1/4 teaspoon coarse ground black pepper
- 3 tablespoons olive oil
- 1/4 teaspoon salt

Directions

- Fill a large saucepan 3/4 full of water and stir in curry powder until dispersed. Add pasta and cook according to package directions, omitting any salt. Drain well, cool with cold running water, and drain again; place in a large serving bowl. Add shrimp, salmon, and asparagus. In a small bowl, stir together the tarragon, lemon juice, salt, and pepper. Using a whisk, briskly whisk in the oil while pouring it in a steady stream. Pour dressing over pasta and toss gently to coat well. Serve right away. Slightly warm leftovers in the microwave before serving.

Nutrition Information

- Carbohydrates: 23g, Protein: 16g, Fat: 7g, Saturated Fat: 1g, Sodium: 450mg, Fiber: 2g

9. Dilled Salmon Pasta With Asparagus

Preparation Time: 30 Minutes

Ingredients

- 2 tablespoons margarine
- 2 tablespoons olive oil
- 1/2 medium red onion, sliced
- 1 pound fresh asparagus, trimmed and cut diagonally into 1-inch lengths
- 4 ounces smoked salmon, sliced into thin strips
- 1/4 teaspoon ground black pepper

- 16 ounces tubular pasta (such as penne or ziti)
- 2 tablespoons chopped fresh dill

Directions

- Heat the margarine and oil in a large skillet. Add the onion and cook, stirring over low heat until tender, about 5 minutes. Add the asparagus and sauté until crisp-tender, about 5 minutes. Add the salmon to the skillet. Sprinkle with pepper, and stir the mixture to blend. Bring a large pot of water to boil and cook the pasta until al dente, about 8–10 minutes. Drain pasta and return it to the cooking pot. Add the asparagus mixture. Stir in the dill and toss to blend.

Nutrition Information

- Carbohydrates: 46g, Protein: 11g, Fat: 8g, Saturated Fat: 1g, Sodium: 148mg, Fiber: 3g

10. Sun-Dried Tomato Seasoned Salmon

Preparation Time: 5 Minutes

Marinating Time: 30 Minutes

Baking Time: 18–21 Minutes

Ingredients

- 2 eight-ounce salmon fillets (about 1 1/2 inches thick
- 1/4 cup purchased sun-dried tomato vinaigrette
- Cooking spray

Directions

- Place salmon fillets in a zip-top bag and pour vinaigrette over them. Seal bag and shake gently to coat. Marinate for 30 minutes in the refrigerator.
- Preheat oven to 450°F. Coat a baking dish with cooking spray. Place salmon in the baking dish with the skin side down. Pour marinade over salmon. Bake uncovered until fish flakes, about 18–21 minutes (6–7 minutes per 1/2-inch thickness of the fillet). Remove skin and cut each fillet in half.

Nutrition Information

- Carbohydrates: 1g, Protein: 23g, Fat: 6g, Saturated Fat: 1g, Sodium: 220mg

11. Simple Grilled Salmon For Diabetics

Preparation Time: 2 Minutes

Cooking Time: About 12 Minutes (May Be Increased Or Decreased Depending On Fillet's Thickness).

Ingredients

- 1/4 teaspoon olive oil
- 1 (4-ounce) salmon fillet
- Pinch of salt
- Pinch of lemon pepper
- Wedge of lemon

Directions

- Preheat grill to medium heat. Rub olive oil over salmon, coating evenly. Sprinkle with salt and lemon pepper. Grill salmon over medium heat for about 6 minutes on each side, or until it flakes easily when pierced with a fork (for ease in turning salmon, a grill basket coated with cooking spray or a wide metal spatula can be used). Remove any skin. Serve with a squeeze of fresh lemon juice.

Nutrition Information

- Carbohydrates: 1g, Protein: 23g, Fat: 5g, Saturated Fat: 1g, Sodium: 240mg, Fiber: <1g

12. Girl Chef's Grilled Lobster

Total Time: 1 Hour 20 Minutes

Ingredients

- 1/2 pound 16–20 count shrimp
- 2 cloves garlic, smashed and finely chopped
- Extra virgin olive oil
- Kosher salt
- Two 1 1/4 to 1 1/2 pound lobsters
- 1 lemon, cut in half
- 4 ears of corn
- 1-pint cherry tomatoes, cut in half
- 1/2 small red onion, thinly sliced
- 6 tablespoons red wine vinegar
- 5 fresh basil leaves, cut into chiffonade

Directions

- In a large bowl, toss the shrimp with the garlic, 2 tablespoons olive oil, and a generous sprinkle of salt. Let the shrimp sit at room temperature for 30 minutes.
- Bring a large pot of well-salted water to a boil. Squeeze both halves of the lemon into the water and drop in the lemon halves.
- Plunge the lobsters into the water, cover, and cook for 4 minutes. Carefully remove the lobsters from the water and

let them cool. The lobsters will NOT be cooked through at this point.

- Preheat a grill to medium.
- Cover half the grill with 2 layers of aluminum foil and place the shrimp in a single layer on the foil (this will prevent the shrimp from falling through the grates). Grill the shrimp on both sides, until pink and opaque, 2 to 3 minutes per side. Remove the shrimp and transfer it to a large bowl.
- While the shrimp are cooking, use the other half of the grill to cook the corn until charred on all sides, about 10 minutes. Remove the corn and let cool. Cut the corn off the cob and add it to the bowl with the shrimp. Holding the corn vertically on your cutting board, run your knife up the cobs to get the lovely little remnants of the corn kernels and add these to the bowl as well. Be sure to get these…they are sweet and delicious and not to be missed!
- Toss the cherry tomatoes and onions with the shrimp and corn. Add the vinegar and a few drops of olive oil. Stir to combine and season with salt. Taste and reseason if needed. Reserve.
- Twist the claws of the lobsters and set them aside. Using a large, very sharp knife, cut the lobsters in half lengthwise. Commit to this you can do it! Remove the contents of the cavity and discard. Save the tomalley (the green stuff) and the coral (the red stuff), for another purpose if desired.

- Place the lobster's cut side down on the grill along with the claws. Grill the lobster for 10 minutes and the claws for 15 minutes, being sure to turn the claws halfway through cooking.
- Transfer the lobsters to serving plates 2 halves, cut side up, and 2 claws per plate. To serve, add the basil to the shrimp corn mixture and spoon it into the cavity of each lobster.

Nutrition Information

- Carbohydrates: 25g, Protein: 25g, Fat: 10g, Saturated Fat: 1g, Cholesterol: 150mg, Sodium: 479mg, Fiber: 3g

13. Grilled Sea Scallops With a Watermelon Three-Way & Dandelion Greens

Total Time: 1 Hour

Ingredients

- 1-pound wedge watermelon
- 1 cup champagne or white wine vinegar
- 2 tablespoons sugar
- 2 tablespoons kosher salt, plus more for seasoning
- Pinch of crushed red pepper
- 8 large sea scallops

- 2 to 3 tablespoons extra virgin olive oil, plus more as needed
- 1 watermelon radish (about the size of a kiwi), peeled and julienned
- 1 cup dandelion greens, cut into 1/2 inch-wide ribbons
- 1/2 small red onion, thinly sliced

Directions

- Carefully cut the rind off the watermelon. Using a mandolin or a sharp vegetable peeler, shave the rind into wide ribbons about 1/8 inch thick. In a large bowl, combine the vinegar, sugar, salt, and red pepper. Add the watermelon rind ribbons and let stand at room temperature for at least an hour (BTW – this can be done yesterday).
- Meanwhile, dice the watermelon flesh into 1/2-inch pieces and reserve.
- When the watermelon pickles are done, heat the grill.
- Brush the scallops with olive oil and season with salt. Place on the grill and cook until grill marks appear, about 1 minute, then rotate the scallops 90 degrees and let the grill marks develop in the other direction (what you're going for here are those lovely crosshatch grill marks!). Turn the scallops over and repeat; the scallops are done when they're no longer translucent, about 2 minutes on each side.

- While the scallops cook, drain the rind pickles, reserving their liquid. Toss the reserved watermelon, the rind pickles, watermelon radish, dandelion greens, and red onion together in a large bowl. Dress the salad with 2 tablespoons of pickling liquid and some olive oil. TASTE! Adjust seasonings and dressing if needed.
- Arrange the deliciously dressed salad in a tall pile just off the center of the four salad plates. Cut the scallops equatorially (through the middle, like the equator) and lay the disks slightly overlapping, grill side up, on the salad. Drizzle with a little olive oil.

Nutrition Information

- Carbohydrates: 19g, Protein: 5g, Fat: 8g, Saturated Fat: 1g, Cholesterol: 7mg, Sodium: 296mg, Fiber: 3g

14. Blackened Shrimp With Tomatoes And Red Onion

Total Time: 30 Minutes

Ingredients

- 1 1/2 teaspoons paprika
- 1 teaspoon Italian seasoning
- 1/2 teaspoon garlic powder
- 1/4 teaspoon black pepper
- 1/2 pound (about 24) small raw shrimp, peeled (with tails on)
- 1 tablespoon canola oil
- 1/2 cup sliced red onion, separated into rings
- 1 1/2 cups halved grape tomatoes
- Lime wedges (optional)

Directions

- Combine paprika, Italian seasoning, garlic powder, and pepper in a small bowl; add to resealable food storage bag. Add shrimp, seal bag, and shake to coat.
- Coat large skillet with nonstick cooking spray; heat over medium-high heat. Heat oil then adds shrimp and cook, turning occasionally, 4 minutes or until shrimp are pink and opaque. Add onion and tomatoes; cook, mixing

occasionally, 1 minute or until tomatoes are hot and onion is slightly wilted. Serve with lime wedges, if desired.

Nutrition Information

- Carbohydrates: 5g, Protein: 13g, Fat: 5g, Saturated Fat: 1g, Cholesterol: 86mg, Sodium: 88mg, Fiber: 1g

15. Spinach, Crab, And Artichoke Dip

Total Time:

Ingredients

- 1 can (6 1/2 ounces) crabmeat, drained and shredded
- 1 package (10 ounces) frozen chopped spinach, thawed and squeezed nearly dry
- 1 package (8 ounces) reduced-fat cream cheese
- 1 jar (about 6 ounces) marinated artichoke hearts, drained and finely chopped
- 1/4 teaspoon hot pepper sauce

- Melba toast or whole-grain crackers (optional)

Directions

- Pick out and discard any shell or cartilage from crabmeat. Combine crabmeat, spinach, cream cheese, artichokes, and hot pepper sauce in a 1 1/2-quart slow cooker. Cover; cook on high 1 1/2 to 2 hours or until heated through, stirring after 1 hour. Serve with melba toast, if desired.

Nutrition Information

- Carbohydrates: 3g, Protein: 6g, Fat: 7g, Saturated Fat: 3g, Cholesterol: 29mg, Sodium: 295mg, Fiber: 1g

16. Southern Crab Cakes With Rémoulade Dipping Sauce

Total Time: 30 Minutes

Ingredients

- 10 ounces fresh lump crabmeat
- 1 1/2 cups fresh white or sourdough bread crumbs, divided

- 1/4 cup chopped green onions
- 1/2 cup fat-free or reduced-fat mayonnaise, divided
- 1 egg white, lightly beaten
- 2 tablespoons coarse-grained or spicy brown mustard, divided
- 3/4 teaspoon hot pepper sauce, divided
- 2 teaspoons olive oil, divided
- Lemon wedges (optional)

Directions

- Preheat oven to 200°F. Pick out and discard any shell or cartilage from crabmeat. Combine crabmeat, 3/4 cup bread crumbs, and green onions in a medium bowl. Add 1/4 cup mayonnaise, egg white, 1 tablespoon mustard, and 1/2 teaspoon hot pepper sauce; mix well. Using 1/4 cup mixture per cake, shape into 8 (1/2-inch-thick) cakes. Roll crab cakes lightly in the remaining 3/4 cup bread crumbs.
- Heat a large nonstick skillet over medium heat; add 1 teaspoon oil. Add 4 crab cakes; cook 4 to 5 minutes per side or until golden brown. Transfer to serving platter; keep warm in the oven. Repeat with the remaining 1 teaspoon oil and crab cakes.
- For the dipping sauce, combine the remaining 1/4 cup mayonnaise, 1 tablespoon mustard, and 1/4 teaspoon hot pepper sauce in a small bowl; mix well.

- Serve crab cakes warm with dipping sauce and lemon wedges, if desired.

Nutrition Information

- Carbohydrates: 8g, Protein: 7g, Fat: 2g, Saturated Fat: 1g, Cholesterol: 30mg, Sodium: 376mg, Fiber: 1g

17. Shrimp Caprese Pasta

Total Time:30 Minutes

Ingredients

- 1 cup uncooked whole wheat penne
- 2 teaspoons olive oil
- 2 cups coarsely chopped grape tomatoes
- 4 tablespoons chopped fresh basil, divided
- 1 tablespoon balsamic vinegar
- 2 cloves garlic, minced
- 1/4 teaspoon salt
- 1/8 teaspoon red pepper flakes
- 8 ounces medium raw shrimp (with tails on), peeled and deveined
- 1 cup grape tomatoes, halved
- 2 ounces fresh mozzarella pearls

Directions

- Cook pasta according to package directions, omitting salt. Drain, reserving 1/2 cup cooking water. Set aside.
- Heat oil in a large skillet over medium heat. Add 2 cups chopped tomatoes, reserving 1/2 cup pasta water, 2 tablespoons basil, vinegar, garlic, salt, and red pepper flakes. Cook and stir 10 minutes or until tomatoes begin to soften.

- Add shrimp and 1 cup halved tomatoes to skillet; cook and stir 5 minutes or until shrimp turn pink and opaque. Add pasta; cook until heated through.
- Divide mixture evenly among four bowls. Top evenly with cheese and the remaining 2 tablespoons of basil.

Nutrition Information

- Carbohydrates: 15g, Protein: 5g, Fat: 2g, Saturated Fat: 1g, Cholesterol: 2mg, Sodium: 160mg, Fiber: 1g

18. Scallop And Artichoke Heart Casserole

Total Time: 50-60 Minutes

Ingredients

- 1 package (9 ounces) frozen artichoke hearts, cooked and drained
- 1 pound scallops
- 1 teaspoon canola or vegetable oil
- 1/4 cup chopped red bell pepper
- 1/4 cup sliced green onions
- 1/4 cup all-purpose flour

- 2 cups low-fat (1%) milk
- 1 teaspoon dried tarragon
- 1/4 teaspoon salt
- 1/4 teaspoon white pepper
- 1 tablespoon chopped fresh parsley
- Dash paprika

Directions

- Preheat oven to 350°F.
- Cut large artichoke hearts lengthwise into halves. Arrange artichoke hearts in an even layer in 8-inch square baking dish.
- Rinse scallops; pat dry with a paper towel. If scallops are large, cut them into halves. Arrange scallops evenly over artichokes.
- Heat oil in a medium saucepan over medium-low heat. Add bell pepper and green onions; cook and stir 5 minutes or until tender. Stir in flour. Gradually stir in milk until smooth. Add tarragon, salt, and white pepper; cook and stir over medium heat 10 minutes or until sauce boils and thickens. Pour sauce over scallops.
- Bake, uncovered, for 25 minutes or until bubbling and scallops are opaque. Sprinkle with parsley and paprika before serving.

Nutrition Information

- Carbohydrates: 23g, Protein: 26g, Fat: 4g, Saturated Fat: 1g, Cholesterol: 43mg, Sodium: 438mg, Fiber: 4g

19. Barbecued Shrimp Over Tropical Rice

Total Time: 30 Minutes

Ingredients

- 20 frozen large raw shrimp, peeled and deveined (26 to 30 per pound)
- 1/2 cup uncooked brown rice
- 1/2 cup barbecue sauce
- 2 teaspoons fresh grated ginger
- 1 cup chopped fresh mango (about 1 medium mango)
- 2 tablespoons finely chopped red onion
- 1 tablespoon chopped fresh cilantro
- 1 tablespoon finely chopped and seeded jalapeño pepper
- 2 teaspoons lime juice

Directions

- Thaw shrimp according to package directions.
- Cook brown rice according to package directions, omitting salt; set aside.
- Meanwhile, thread shrimp onto 4 metal skewers, leaving 1/8-inch space between shrimp. In a small bowl stir together barbecue sauce and ginger. Grill shrimp on the greased rack of an uncovered grill directly over medium

heat for 6 to 7 minutes or until shrimp are opaque, turning once and brushing frequently with sauce mixture.

- Stir mango, onion, cilantro, jalapeño, and lime juice into hot rice. Spoon onto serving plates. Serve shrimp on top of the rice mixture.

Nutrition Information

- Carbohydrates: 37g, Protein: 9g, Fat: 2g, Saturated Fat: 1g, Cholesterol: 53mg, Sodium: 396mg, Fiber: 2g

20. Shrimp & Caper Vermicelli

foxeslovelemons.com

Total Time: 20-30 Minutes

Ingredients

- 1 medium tomato, seeded and chopped
- 1/4 cup chopped parsley
- 3 tablespoons capers, rinsed and drained
- 2 tablespoons dry white wine or low-sodium broth
- 1 1/2 tablespoons extra virgin olive oil
- 1 clove garlic, minced
- 1/2 teaspoon grated lemon peel
- 2 tablespoons lemon juice

- 1/4 teaspoon salt
- 1/8 to 1/4 teaspoon red pepper flakes
- 6 ounces uncooked dry vermicelli, broken in thirds
- 10 ounces peeled fresh or frozen and thawed raw medium shrimp
- 2 ounces reduced-fat feta, crumbled (plain or basil and sun-dried tomato variety)

Directions

- Combine tomato, parsley, capers, wine, lemon juice, oil, garlic, lemon peel, salt, and red pepper flakes in a large bowl; set aside.
- Cook pasta according to directions on the package, omitting any salt or fat. After 6 minutes of cooking, add shrimp to pasta. Return to a boil and cook 4 to 5 minutes or until shrimp is pink and opaque. Drain well. Add to tomato mixture, and toss well.
- Place shrimp mixture in a pasta bowl or place equal amounts on each of four dinner plates. Sprinkle evenly with cheese.

Nutrition Information

- Carbohydrates: 35g| Protein: 23g| Fat: 9g| Saturated Fat: 2g| Cholesterol: 113mg| Sodium: 646mg| Fiber: 2g

21. Shrimp and Watermelon Ceviche

Total Time: 1 Hour 45 Minutes

Ingredients

- 1 pound medium raw shrimp, peeled and deveined
- 1/2 cup plus 2 tablespoons lime juice, divided
- 1 cup finely chopped seedless watermelon

- 1/2 cup finely chopped jicama
- 1/2 cup finely chopped red onion
- 1/2 cup chopped fresh cilantro
- 1 jalapeño pepper, minced
- 56 water crackers

Directions

- Remove tails from shrimp; discard. Chop shrimp into small pieces.
- Combine shrimp and 1/2 cup lime juice in a medium bowl. Cover and refrigerate for 1 hour or until shrimp are pink and opaque. Drain; discard juice.
- Meanwhile, combine watermelon, jicama, onion, cilantro, jalapeño, and the remaining 2 tablespoons lime juice in a large bowl. Gently stir in shrimp. Cover and refrigerate for at least 30 minutes to allow flavors to develop.
- Serve on or with water crackers.

Nutrition Information

- Carbohydrates: 7g, Protein: 3g, Fat: 1g, Cholesterol: 20mg, Sodium: 132mg, Fiber: 1g

22. Pesto Pasta With Scallops

Total Time: 30 Minutes

Ingredients

- 8 ounces whole-wheat rotini or other curly whole wheat pasta
- 5 1/2 teaspoons olive oil, divided
- 12 ounces asparagus (about 20 asparagus), cut into 2-inch-pieces
- 8 ounces cherry tomatoes, halved (about 2 cups)
- 1/2 teaspoon black pepper, divided
- 12 ounces large sea scallops
- 1 tablespoon lemon juice
- 1 clove garlic, crushed
- 1/4 teaspoon salt
- 6 tablespoons prepared pesto
- 3 tablespoons fat-free sour cream
- Pinch red pepper flakes (optional)
- Fresh basil for garnish

Directions

- Prepare pasta according to package directions, omitting any salt or fat. Set aside and keep warm.
- Meanwhile, heat 1 1/2 teaspoon's oil in a medium skillet over medium heat. Cook asparagus for 5 minutes, stirring

occasionally. Toss in tomatoes and turn heat to low. Sprinkle with 1/4 teaspoon black pepper, cover, and continue cooking for about 5 additional minutes. (Stir occasionally to prevent sticking.) Add asparagus and tomatoes to pasta and keep warm.

- Toss scallops with 1 teaspoon oil, lemon juice, garlic, and 1/4 teaspoon black pepper in a large bowl. (Do not marinate.)

- In the same skillet, heat the remaining 1 tablespoon oil over medium-high heat. Add scallops and sprinkle with salt. Cook about 3 minutes per side until scallops are opaque.

- Combine pesto and sour cream in a small bowl; add to vegetable and pasta mixture, mix well. Add red pepper flakes, if desired. Arrange scallops on top and garnish with fresh basil.

Nutrition Information

- Carbohydrates: 37g, Protein: 17g, Fat: 11g, Saturated Fat: 1g, Cholesterol: 19mg, Sodium: 383mg, Fiber: 5g

23. Hot Shrimp With Cool Salsa

Total Time:20 Minutes

Ingredients

- 1/4 cup salsa
- 4 tablespoons fresh lime juice, divided
- 1 teaspoon honey
- 1 clove garlic, minced
- 2 to 4 drops hot pepper sauce
- 1 pound large shrimp, peeled and deveined, with tails intact

- 1 cup finely diced honeydew melon
- 1/2 cup finely diced unpeeled cucumber
- 2 tablespoons minced parsley
- 1 green onion, finely chopped
- 1 1/2 teaspoons sugar
- 1 teaspoon olive oil
- 1/4 teaspoon salt

Directions

- To make a marinade, combine salsa, 2 tablespoons lime juice, honey, garlic, and hot pepper sauce in a small bowl. Thread shrimp onto skewers. Brush shrimp with marinade; set aside.
- To make salsa, combine the remaining 2 tablespoons of lime juice, melon, cucumber, parsley, onion, sugar, oil, and salt in a medium bowl; mix well.
- Grill shrimp over medium coals for 4 to 5 minutes or until shrimp turn pink, turning once. Serve with salsa.

Nutrition Information

- Carbohydrates: 8g, Protein: 19g, Fat: 2g, Saturated Fat: 1g, Cholesterol: 175mg, Sodium: 398mg, Fiber: 1g

24. Fresh Garlic Shrimp Linguine

Total Time: 20 Minutes

Ingredients

- 6 ounces uncooked multigrain linguine or spaghetti, broken in half
- 1/2 pound raw shrimp, peeled and deveined
- 1/4 cup grated Parmesan cheese
- 3 tablespoons diet margarine
- 1 clove garlic, minced
- 1/2 teaspoon seafood seasoning
- 1/4 cup finely chopped fresh parsley (optional)
- 1/8 teaspoon salt (optional)

Directions

- Cook linguine according to package directions, omitting salt and fat, about 7 minutes or until al dente. Add shrimp; cook 3 to 4 minutes or until shrimp are pink and opaque. Drain; transfer to a medium bowl. Add cheese, margarine, garlic, and seafood seasoning; toss gently to coat. Add parsley and salt, if desired; toss to combine.

Nutrition Information

- Carbohydrates: 30g, Protein: 21g, Fat: 7g, Saturated Fat: 2g, Cholesterol: 91mg, Sodium: 242mg, Fiber: 3g

25. Warm Shrimp, Artichoke, And Parmesan Salad

Total Time: 20 Minutes

Ingredients

- 1 can (14 ounces) water-packed quartered artichoke hearts
- 20 frozen cooked tail-on premium shrimp (12 ounces)
- 1/2 cup fat-free Italian salad dressing
- 1 bag (12 ounces) salad blend
- 1/4 cup (1 ounce) shredded Parmesan cheese

Directions

- Drain and rinse artichoke hearts. Combine with shrimp and dressing in a large, deep skillet. Cover and cook over medium heat for 10 minutes, stirring occasionally.
- Divide salad blend among 4 dinner plates. Top salad with the shrimp-artichoke mixture. Sprinkle with cheese.

Nutrition Information

- Carbohydrates: 21g, Protein: 24g, Fat: 3g, Saturated Fat: 1g, Cholesterol: 133mg, Sodium: 757mg, Fiber: 7g

26. Spicy Fish Tacos

Cook Time: 10 Min

What You'll Need

- 1/2 cup reduced-fat mayonnaise
- 1/4 cup reduced-fat sour cream
- 1 teaspoon hot sauce
- 2 tablespoons lemon juice
- 2 (8-ounce) tilapia fillets or other firm-fleshed fish fillets
- 1/8 teaspoon cayenne pepper
- 1/4 teaspoon onion powder
- 4 (6-inch) flour tortillas
- 1 cup shredded red cabbage

What To Do

- Preheat oven to broil. Line a broiler pan with aluminum foil; coat with cooking spray.
- In a medium bowl, whisk together mayonnaise, sour cream, hot sauce, and lemon juice. Refrigerate sauce until ready to use.
- Sprinkle fish on both sides with cayenne pepper and onion powder.
- Broil fillets about 5 inches from heat for 3-5 minutes on each side or until fish flakes easily. Cut fillets in half lengthwise.

- On each tortilla, place half a fillet, 1/4 cup shredded cabbage, and 2 tablespoons sauce. Roll or fold the tortilla. Serve immediately.

Nutritional Information

- Total Fat: 16g| Saturated Fat: 3.9g| Protein: 27g| Cholesterol: 72mg| Sodium: 513mg| Total Carbohydrates: 21g| Dietary Fiber: 1.1g| Sugars: 3.6g

27. Greek Festival Fish

Cook Time: 20 Min

What You'll Need

- 2 tablespoons olive oil
- 8 scallions, thinly sliced
- 2 cloves garlic, minced
- 4 tomatoes, chopped
- 1/2 cup dry white wine
- 2 tablespoons finely chopped parsley
- 1 teaspoon dried oregano
- 1 teaspoon black pepper
- 6 white-fleshed fish fillets (2 pounds total) such as tilapia, flounder, or sole
- 1 (4-ounce) package crumbled feta cheese

What To Do

- Preheat the oven to 400 degrees. Coat a 9-inch by a 13-inch baking dish with cooking spray.
- In a medium skillet, heat the oil over medium heat. Add the scallions and garlic and sauté until tender. Add the tomatoes, wine, parsley, oregano, and pepper. Simmer for 5 minutes, or until the sauce thickens. Remove from the heat.

- Place half of the sauce mixture in the baking dish. Arrange the fish fillets over the sauce and cover them with the remaining sauce. Sprinkle with the feta cheese.
- Bake for 15 to 18 minutes, or until the fish flakes easily with a fork. Serve immediately.

Nutritional Information

- Total Fat: 18g| Saturated Fat: 5.6g| Trans Fat: 0.1g| Protein: 28g| Cholesterol: 104mg| Sodium: 375mg| Total Carbohydrates: 5.9g| Dietary Fiber: 1.5g| Sugars: 3.1g

28. Almond Crusted Fish Fillets

Cook Time: 30 Min

What You'll Need

- 1 tablespoon sugar
- 3/4 teaspoon ground cinnamon
- 1/4 teaspoon ground red pepper
- 1/2 teaspoon salt
- 1 1/2 pound white-fleshed fish fillets
- 1 egg white, beaten
- 2 cups sliced almonds
- 2 tablespoons butter, plus more as needed
- 1/4 cup olive oil, plus more as needed
- 1/2 cup Amaretto liqueur

What To Do

- In a small bowl, combine sugar, cinnamon, red pepper, and salt; mix well. Season fillets with 1 teaspoon of the mixture, reserving the remaining mixture.
- Place egg white in a shallow dish; place almonds in another shallow dish. Dip each fillet in egg white then in almonds, coating completely.
- In a large skillet, melt butter with oil over medium heat. Add half of the fillets and cook 5 minutes then turn fillets and cook 2 to 3 more minutes, or until fish flakes easily with a fork; transfer to a serving platter and cover to keep warm. Repeat with remaining fillets, adding additional butter and oil as needed.
- Add reserved sugar mixture and amaretto to skillet; reduce heat to low and cook 1 to 2 minutes, or until thickened, stirring constantly. Pour over fillets and serve immediately.

Nutritional Information

- Total Fat: 43g| Saturated Fat: 7.6g| Trans Fat: 0.2g| Protein: 42g|Cholesterol: 139mg| Sodium: 506mg| Total Carbohydrates: 31g|Dietary Fiber: 5.9g| Sugars: 8.1g

29. Florentine Fish Roll-Ups

Prep Time: 10 Mins

Cook Time: 18 Mins

What You'll Need

- 1 (10-ounce) package frozen chopped spinach, thawed and well-drained
- 2 tablespoons grated Parmesan cheese
- 1/4 teaspoon garlic powder
- 1/4 teaspoon salt
- 1/4 teaspoon black pepper
- 4 (6-ounce) white-fleshed fish fillets, such as sole, flounder, or tilapia
- Cooking spray
- 1/2 teaspoon paprika

What To Do

- Preheat the oven to 350 degrees. Coat a rimmed baking sheet with cooking spray.
- In a medium bowl, combine the spinach, Parmesan cheese, garlic powder, salt, and pepper; mix well.
- Spread the spinach mixture evenly over the fish fillets. Roll up jellyroll style and place seam side down on the baking sheet.

- Lightly coat the fish with the cooking spray and sprinkle with the paprika. Bake for 18 to 22 minutes, or until the fish flakes easily with a fork.

Nutritional Information

- Total Fat: 11g| Saturated Fat: 2.7g| Trans Fat: 0.1g| Protein: 30g| Cholesterol: 96mg| Sodium: 403mg| Total Carbohydrates: 3.4g| Dietary Fiber: 2.2g| Sugars: 0.5g

30. Fiesta Fish Tacos

Total Time: 30 Minutes

What You'll Need

- Juice of 1/2 lime
- 2 cloves garlic, minced
- 1 tablespoon olive oil
- 1 pound tilapia fillets
- 1/2 cup chopped green bell pepper
- 1/2 cup chopped red bell pepper
- 1 tablespoon minced cilantro
- 1 cup cherry or grape tomatoes
- 4 (6-inch) whole-wheat tortillas

- 2 cups shredded lettuce
- 1 cup cubed mango
- Black pepper, to taste

What To Do

- Mix lime juice, garlic, and olive oil in a glass bowl.
- Add tilapia and marinate in the refrigerator for 1 hour.
- Place tilapia in a glass baking dish surrounded by green and red bell pepper, minced cilantro, and tomatoes.
- Bake at 350 degrees F for 10 minutes or until fish flakes easily.
- Divide fish and veggies into 4 servings and place on each of the warmed tortillas.
- Top with lettuce, cubed mango, and a sprinkling of black pepper.
- Before You Start Cooking!

Nutritional Information

- Total Fat: 8.7g| Saturated Fat: 2.2g| Protein: 28g| Cholesterol: 57mg| Sodium: 346mg| Total Carbohydrates: 33g| Dietary Fiber: 5.3g| Sugars: 11g

31. Peppered Shrimp Skewers

Total Time: 45 Minutes

Ingredients

- 1/3 cup teriyaki sauce
- 1/3 cup ketchup
- 2 tablespoons dry sherry or water
- 2 tablespoons reduced-fat peanut butter
- 1 teaspoon hot pepper sauce
- 1/4 teaspoon ground ginger
- 32 large raw shrimp (about 1 1/2 pounds), peeled and deveined, with tails on
- 2 large yellow bell peppers
- 32 fresh sugar snap peas, trimmed

Directions

- Soak 16 (12-inch) wooden skewers in water for at least 20 minutes before assembling kabobs.
- Preheat broiler. Coat rack of broiler pan with nonstick cooking spray; set aside.
- Combine teriyaki sauce, ketchup, sherry, peanut butter, pepper sauce, and ginger in a small saucepan. Bring to a boil, stirring constantly. Reduce heat to low; simmer, uncovered, 1 minute. Remove from heat; set aside.

- Cut each bell pepper lengthwise into 4 quarters; remove stems and seeds. Cut each quarter crosswise into 4 equal pieces. Thread 2 shrimp, 2 bell pepper pieces, and 2 sugar snap peas onto each skewer; place on prepared pan. Brush with teriyaki sauce mixture.
- Broil skewers 4 inches from heat 3 minutes; turn. Brush with teriyaki sauce mixture; broil 2 minutes or until shrimp turn pink and opaque. Discard any remaining teriyaki sauce mixture.

Nutrition Information

- Carbohydrates: 7g, Protein: 10g, Fat: 2g, Saturated Fat: 1g, Cholesterol: 66mg, Sodium: 245mg, Fiber: 1g

32. Sautéed Shrimp Recipe For Diabetics

Preparation Time: 10 Minutes

Cooking Time: 5 Minutes

Ingredients

- 4 sun-dried tomato halves
- 1/4 cup hot water
- 1 tablespoon olive oil
- 1/2 pound cooked and peeled shrimp (20–24 count size)
- 1 cup baby spinach leaves, rinsed and drained
- 1 teaspoon dried basil

- 1/4 teaspoon black pepper

Directions

- Place sun-dried tomato halves into a small bowl. Pour hot water over the tomatoes and set aside for 10 minutes, stirring occasionally. After 10 minutes, remove tomatoes from the water, reserving the water for later use. Chop tomatoes and set them aside. In a large sauté pan, heat olive oil. Add cooked shrimp and sauté. Add chopped tomato and spinach, then pour in the 1/4 cup reserved hot water and continue cooking. Add dried basil and black pepper, stir until combined, and serve immediately.

Nutrition Information

- Carbohydrates: 4g, Protein: 25g, Fat: 8g, Saturated Fat: 2g, Cholesterol: 221mg, Sodium: 346mg, Fiber: 1g

33. Spicy Shrimp Appetizers

Preparation Time: 2 Minutes

Cooking Time: 10 Minutes

Ingredients

- 2 quarts water
- 1 pound shelled and cooked medium frozen shrimp (21–24 count)
- 1/4 cup no-added-salt tomato paste
- 1/2 teaspoon minced garlic
- 1/2 teaspoon crushed red pepper
- 1 teaspoon olive oil

- 1 teaspoon basil
- 1/4 teaspoon black pepper
- 2–3 drops hot pepper sauce
- 24 toothpicks
- 3 leaf lettuce leaves for presentation

Directions

- Bring 2 quarts of water to a boil in a large saucepan over medium heat. Add frozen shrimp and cook approximately 3 minutes until shrimp are heated through. Drain.
- In a small bowl, whisk together tomato paste, garlic, crushed red pepper, olive oil, basil, black pepper, and hot sauce. Pour mixture into a large skillet and heat at low heat, stirring constantly. Add hot, cooked shrimp and stir to coat with sauce. Place 1 toothpick in each shrimp. Serve immediately on a large plate covered with 3 lettuce leaves.

Nutrition Information

- Carbohydrates: 2g, Protein: 14g, Fat: 2g, Saturated Fat: 1g, Cholesterol: 112mg, Sodium: 65mg

34. Triple-quick Shrimp And Pasta

Total Time:

Ingredients

- 4 ounces uncooked whole grain rotini pasta
- 8 ounces small shrimp (with tails), peeled
- 4 ounces asparagus spears, trimmed and broken into 2-inch pieces
- 1 cup grape tomatoes, quartered
- 1/2 cup light olive oil vinaigrette
- 2 cloves garlic, minced
- 2 teaspoons chopped fresh rosemary
- 1/4 cup chopped fresh basil

- 1/4 cup grated Parmesan cheese

Directions

- Cook pasta according to package directions, omitting salt and fat. Add shrimp during the last 4 minutes of cooking. Add asparagus during the last 3 minutes of cooking; cook until shrimp are pink and opaque. Drain and return to saucepan.
- Add tomatoes, vinaigrette, garlic, and rosemary. Toss until well blended. Stir in basil and Parmesan cheese.

Nutrition Information

- Carbohydrates: 27g, Protein: 16g, Fat: 7g, Saturated Fat: 1g, Cholesterol: 76mg, Sodium: 766mg, Fiber: 3g

35. Crab Soup

Preparation Time: 15 Minutes

Cooking Time: 25 Minutes

Ingredients

- 1 can (10 3/4 ounces) Campbell's Healthy Request Cream of Chicken soup
- 1 1/2 cups water
- 1/4 cup skim milk
- 1/2 pound Yukon Gold potatoes, washed and peeled
- 2 ounces whole white mushrooms (about 2 large)
- 1 can (6 ounces) lump crabmeat, drained
- 2 tablespoons chopped red bell pepper
- 1/4 teaspoon black pepper
- 1/4 teaspoon onion powder

Directions

- In a 2-quart saucepan, combine soup, water, and milk and stir well to combine into a smooth mixture. Place the saucepan on the stove over medium heat. Finely dice potatoes (should yield about 1 1/4 cups) and add to liquid. Remove stems from mushrooms and wipe away visible dirt with a small brush or paper towel. Chop mushrooms and add to saucepan, along with drained crabmeat, bell pepper, black pepper, and onion powder. Bring to a gentle boil, then cover and simmer for approximately 15 minutes until potatoes are soft, then serve.

Nutrition Information

- Carbohydrates: 18g, Protein: 8g, Fat: 2g, Saturated Fat: 1g, Cholesterol: 3mg, Sodium: 485mg, Fiber: 2g

36. Greek Shrimp

Preparation Time: 40 Minutes

Ingredients

- 1 tablespoon olive oil
- 1 large onion, chopped
- 1/4 cup chopped fresh parsley
- 1 clove garlic, minced
- 1/2 teaspoon sugar
- 1 1/2 pounds roma tomatoes, peeled and chopped
- 1 cup dry white wine

- 1 pound cooked medium-size shrimp, peeled and deveined (frozen, fully cooked shrimp, thawed, may be used for convenience)
- 1/4 cup grated mizithra cheese

Directions

- Warm the oil in a large, nonstick skillet over medium heat. Add onion and sauté until tender, about 3–4 minutes. Stir in parsley, garlic, and sugar. Add tomatoes and cook uncovered until they soften and the liquid evaporates about 8–10 minutes; stir frequently. Add wine and cook until liquid evaporates about 10 minutes. Add shrimp and cook, stirring occasionally, for 2–3 minutes, or until shrimp are heated through. Transfer to a serving dish and top with cheese. Can be served over cooked brown rice.

Nutrition Information

- Carbohydrates: 15g, Protein: 21g, Fat: 5g, Saturated Fat: 1g, Sodium: 528mg, Fiber: 2g

37. Classic Gumbo

Preparation Time: 3 Hours

Ingredients

- 1 1/2 quarts water
- 8 ounces crabmeat
- 5 ounces shrimp
- 2 bay leaves
- 2 lemon wedges
- 2 slices onion
- 1 teaspoon plus 1/2 teaspoon cayenne pepper
- 1 teaspoon black pepper
- 1 tablespoon chopped parsley
- 1 pound okra, sliced
- 4 tablespoons vegetable oil
- 2 medium tomatoes, chopped
- 1 onion, diced
- 1 green pepper, diced
- 2 tablespoons flour
- 1 teaspoon thyme
- 3 1/2 cups prepared white rice

Directions

- In a large pot, bring 1 1/2 quarts water to a boil and add crabmeat, shrimp, bay leaves, lemon wedges, onion slices,

1 teaspoon cayenne pepper, and black pepper. Boil for 10 minutes. Remove shrimp and crabmeat and set in the refrigerator. Strain stock and set aside.

- Sauté sliced okra in 1 tablespoon of vegetable oil in a large skillet. When soft and lightly browned, place in a large pot. Add chopped tomatoes to okra and cook over low heat, stirring often. In a skillet with 1 tablespoon of the vegetable oil sauté green peppers and onion until tender. Add to okra and tomatoes and cook, stirring often. In the skillet, add 2 tablespoons of flour and stir until slightly browned (if it burns, discard flour and start over again). Add the remaining 2 tablespoons of vegetable oil to the flour and stir until the mixture is slightly bubbly. Stir in 1 cup of the reserved stock and cook until thickened. Add this liquid to the pot with vegetables. Stir thoroughly, keeping the heat on low. Add additional stock to create a thick, stewlike consistency. Stir in thyme and 1/2 teaspoon cayenne pepper. Cover and cook over low heat for an additional two hours. Add reserved crabmeat and shrimp to gumbo and blend, adding additional stock if needed. Cover and continue to heat for another 30 minutes. Prepare rice
- To serve, place 1/2 cup boiled white rice in a large soup bowl and top with 1 cup gumbo. Serve immediately.

Nutrition Information

- Carbohydrates: 29g, Protein: 15g, Fat: 9g, Saturated Fat: 1g, Sodium: 146mg, Fiber: 3g

38. Shrimp And Beet Smörgåsor

Preparation Time: 8 Minutes

Ingredients

- 1/4-inch-thick slice French or Italian Bread
- 1 teaspoon reduced-fat margarine spread
- 2 slices canned, chilled pickled beets, drained and blotted on paper towels
- 2 large shrimp, cooked, peeled, deveined, and chilled
- 1 teaspoon chopped green pepper

Directions

- Spread a thin layer of margarine on bread, and layer with pickled beets, shrimp, and green pepper. Serve immediately, as beets may bleed into sandwiches.

Nutrition Information

- Carbohydrates: 23g| Protein: 8g| Fat: 3g| Sodium: 390 mg| Fiber: 2g

39. Shrimp Po'boy

Preparation Time: 20 Minutes

Ingredients

- 1 loaf French bread, about 24 inches long and 2 1/2 inches wide
- 2 cups shredded iceberg lettuce
- 2 medium tomatoes, thinly sliced
- 8 ounces cooked shrimp, chilled

Cajun Remoulade:

- 4 tablespoons fat-free mayonnaise
- 1/2 tablespoon Creole or Dijon mustard
- 1/2 tablespoon sweet pickle relish
- 1 hard-boiled egg, diced
- 2 tablespoons minced onion
- 2 tablespoons chopped fresh parsley
- 1/2 teaspoon Worcestershire sauce
- 1/2 teaspoon salt-free Creole seasoning

Directions

- Cut French bread crosswise into four pieces, each about 6 inches long, and split open each section. Prepare Cajun remoulade by mixing mayonnaise, mustard, relish, egg, onion, parsley, Worcestershire sauce, and Creole seasoning in a small mixing bowl. Chill remoulade while assembling a sandwich. Place French bread sections on a baking sheet and toast in a 375°F oven for 5 minutes. Bread should be crispy, but not browned. Remove from oven and fill each sandwich with 1/2 cup shredded lettuce, 1/4 of the tomato slices, 2 ounces (approximately 1/3 cup) shrimp, and 3 tablespoons Cajun remoulade. Serve immediately.

Nutrition Information

- Carbohydrates: 56g| Protein: 23g| Fat: 6g| Saturated Fat: 1g| Sodium: 899mg| Fiber: 4g

40. Fish Creole

Total Time: 20-30 Minutes

Ingredients

- 4 (3-ounce) fish fillets
- 2 tablespoons lemon juice
- 2 tablespoons finely chopped onion

- 4 tablespoons reduced-fat margarine, divided
- 1/2 cup chopped green peppers
- 1 cup chopped canned tomatoes, undrained
- Pepper to taste
- 2 teaspoons flour

Directions

- Preheat oven to 350 degrees F.
- Place fish fillets in a baking pan coated with nonstick cooking spray.
- Mix lemon juice, onion, and 2 tablespoons of melted margarine. Pour mixture over fish. Bake uncovered or until fish flakes easily with a fork, about 15 minutes.
- While fish is baking, prepare the creole sauce; saute green pepper in the remaining margarine. Add tomatoes and pepper. Stir in flour. Simmer until the mixture is heated.

Nutritional Information

- Fat: 9g| Fiber: 1g| Sodium: 338mg| Cholesterol: 37mg| Protein: 25g| Carbohydrates: 7g| Sugars: 4g

41. Seafood Kabobs

Total Time: 30-60 Minutes

Ingredients

- 2 tablespoons lime juice
- 1 tablespoon olive oil
- 1 clove garlic, crushed
- 1/8 teaspoon salt
- 1/4 teaspoon freshly ground black pepper
- 2 teaspoons fresh snipped dill
- 12 large shelled deveined shrimp (6 ounces meat)
- 7 large sea scallops (6 ounces)
- 1 medium zucchini cut into 1-inch pieces (2 cups)
- 1 medium yellow squash cut into 1-inch pieces (2 cups)

Directions

- Preheat grill or broiler.
- Mix lime juice, olive oil, garlic, salt, pepper, and dill. Add shrimp, scallops, and vegetables and set aside to marinate for 15 minutes. Turn once during this time.
- Alternate vegetables, shrimp, and scallops on 4 skewers. Grill or broil 3-4 inches from the heat source for 2-1/2 minutes per side. Do not overcook the fish. Sprinkle with salt and pepper.

- Place skewers on 2 dinner plates or remove seafood and vegetables from skewers onto 2 plates and serve.

Nutritional Information

- Fat: 5g| Saturated Fat: 7g| Fiber: 4g| Sodium: 314mg| Cholesterol: 157mg| Protein: 34g| Carbohydrates: 12g

42. Primavera Fish Fillets

Total Time: 60 Minutes

Ingredients

- 4 (4-ounce) fresh or frozen orange roughy fillets
- 2 tablespoons unsalted butter
- 1 tablespoon fresh lemon juice
- 1/4 teaspoon freshly ground black pepper
- 1 garlic clove, minced
- 1-1/2 cups fresh broccoli florets
- 1 cup fresh cauliflower florets
- 1 cup julienne-cut carrots
- 1 cup sliced fresh white mushrooms

- 1/2 cup diagonally sliced celery
- 1/8 teaspoon salt
- 1/4 teaspoon dried basil
- 2 tablespoons grated Parmesan cheese

Directions

- Heat the oven to 450 degrees. Thaw roughly if frozen. Place 1 tablespoon butter into a 13x9-inch glass or ceramic baking dish and melt in the oven. Place roughy fillets in melted butter and turn to coat, arranging fillets in a single layer. Sprinkle with lemon juice and pepper. Bake for 5 minutes. Remove from the oven.
- While fish is baking, melt the remaining 1 tablespoon butter in a large skillet over medium-high heat. Add garlic and cook until lightly browned. Add broccoli, cauliflower, carrots, mushrooms, celery, salt, and basil. Cook, stirring, for 5 to 6 minutes or until vegetables are crisp-tender.
- Spoon hot vegetables into the center of the baking dish, moving fish to the sides of the dish. Sprinkle vegetables and fish with Parmesan cheese.
- Return the dish to the oven and bake an additional 3 to 5 minutes or until fish flakes easily with a fork.

Nutritional

- Fat: 11g| Sodium: 216mg| Cholesterol: 38mg| Protein: 28g| Carbohydrates: 7g

43. Fish With Chinese Ginger Scallion Sauce

Total Time: 20-30 Minutes

Ingredients

- 2 Tbsp. canola oil
- 1-1/2 cups thinly sliced scallion, white and green parts
- 2 tsp. grated fresh ginger
- 1/2 tsp. sugar
- 1/4 tsp. salt
- 1 tsp. grated orange zest
- Freshly ground pepper, preferably white, to taste
- 4 (4-oz.) pieces tilapia or other mild, flaky white fish

Directions

- Preheat the broiler.
- Heat oil in a small skillet over medium heat. Mix in scallions to coat them with oil. Add ginger, sugar, and salt. Cook, stirring until sugar dissolves and scallions are tender but still bright green, 3-4 minutes. Off the heat, mix in the zest. Season sauce generously with pepper. Set skillet aside so it keeps warm while the fish cooks.
- Arrange fish on a baking sheet and coat with cooking spray. Season fish lightly with salt and ground pepper.

Broil until fish is opaque in the center at the thickest point, about 6 minutes. Divide fish among four dinner plates. Top each piece with one-fourth of the sauce. Serve immediately.

Nutritional Information

- Fat: 9g| Sodium: 210mg| Protein: 23g| Carbohydrates: 3g

44. Seafood Kabobs Hawaiian

Total Time: 50-60 Minutes

Ingredients

- 1/2 cup dry sherry
- 1 teaspoon sesame oil
- 2 tablespoons grated fresh ginger

- 2 tablespoons tamari soy sauce
- 2 tablespoons pineapple juice concentrate
- 1 pound fresh sea scallops or shrimp, peeled and deveined
- 1 large mango, peeled and cut into wedges
- 1/2 papaya, peeled and cut into wedges
- 1 large red pepper, seeded and cut into large squares

Directions

- In a medium bowl, combine the sherry, sesame oil, ginger, soy sauce, and pineapple juice concentrate. Add the shrimp or scallops. Let the shellfish marinate for 30 minutes in the refrigerator.
- Prepare an outside grill or oven broiler by placing the rack 6 inches from the heat source. Remove the shrimp or scallops from the marinade. Reserve the remaining marinade. Thread the shellfish onto wooden skewers and alternate them with the mango, papaya, and red pepper.
- Place the skewers on the grill and frill for about 5 minutes, turning and basting with the marinade.

Nutritional Information

- Fat: 2g| Sodium: 429mg| Cholesterol: 95g| Protein: 16g| Carbohydrates: 20g

45. Sizzlin' Catfish

Cook Time: 5 Min

What You'll Need

- 2 tablespoons vegetable oil
- 4 (4-ounce) catfish fillets
- 1/8 teaspoon salt
- 1/4 teaspoon black pepper
- 1 tablespoon lemon juice
- 1/4 pound fresh mushrooms, sliced
- 1 onion, chopped
- 1/4 cup chopped fresh parsley

What to Do

- In a large skillet, heat the oil over medium heat.
- Season the catfish fillets with salt and pepper. Add to the skillet and sprinkle with lemon juice. Add the remaining ingredients to the skillet. Cook for 3 to 4 minutes per side, or until the fish flakes easily with a fork.
- Serve the fish topped with vegetables.

Nutritional Information

- Total Fat: 14g| Saturated Fat: 2.4g| Trans Fat: 0.1g| Protein: 18g| Cholesterol: 62mg| Sodium: 188mg| Total Carbohydrates: 3.1g| Dietary Fiber: 0.7g| Sugars: 1.4g

46. Fast 'n' Fiery Grilled Catfish

Cook Time: 15 Min

What You'll Need

- 1 tablespoon chopped fresh basil
- 1 teaspoon crushed red pepper
- 1 teaspoon garlic powder
- 1/2 teaspoon salt
- 1/2 teaspoon black pepper
- 4 (6-ounce) farm-raised catfish fillets
- 2 tablespoons canola oil

What To Do

- Preheat the grill to medium-high heat. Coat a hinged grill basket with nonstick cooking spray.
- In a small bowl, combine the basil, crushed red pepper, garlic powder, salt, and black pepper; mix well.
- Rinse the fish with cold water and pat dry with a paper towel. Rub the oil over both sides of the fish, then rub both sides with the seasoning mixture, coating evenly.
- Place the fish in the grill basket and grill for 7 to 9 minutes, or until cooked through and firm to the touch, turning the basket over once during cooking.

Nutritional Information

- Total Fat: 17g| Saturated Fat: 2.8g|Trans Fat: 0.1g| Protein: 26g| Cholesterol: 94mg| Sodium: 458mg| Total Carbohydrates: 0.7g| Dietary Fiber: 0.2g

47. Sesame-Crusted Swordfish

Cook Time: 10 Min

What You'll Need

- 1/2 cup lemon juice
- 1/4 cup vegetable oil
- 2 cloves garlic, minced
- 1/2 teaspoon salt
- 1/2 teaspoon black pepper
- 4 (4-ounce) swordfish steaks (1/2-inch-thick)
- 2 teaspoons sesame seeds

What To Do

- In a shallow dish, combine all the ingredients except the swordfish and sesame seeds; mix well. Add the swordfish and coat completely. Cover and marinate in the refrigerator for 2 hours, turning occasionally.
- Coat a grill pan with cooking spray and heat over medium-high heat.
- Remove the swordfish from the marinade; discard the marinade. Grill the fish for 4 to 5 minutes; turn the fish, sprinkle with sesame seeds, and grill for 4 to 5 more minutes, or until it flakes easily with a fork. Serve immediately.

Nutritional Information

- Total Fat: 22g| Saturated Fat: 3.7g| Trans Fat: 0.1g| Protein: 23g| Cholesterol: 75mg| Sodium: 384mg| Total Carbohydrates: 2.9g| Dietary Fiber: 0.4g| Sugars: 0.8g

48. Louisiana Broiled Catfish

Cook Time: 12 Min

What You'll Need

- 4 (4-ounce) catfish fillets, rinsed and patted dry
- Cooking spray
- 2 teaspoons Creole seasoning
- 1 lemon, cut into wedges

What To Do

- Preheat broiler. Coat a broiler pan with cooking spray.
- Coat both sides of fillets with cooking spray and sprinkle with seasoning.
- Place fillets on prepared pan about 5 inches from heat. Broil each side for about 6 minutes, or until fish is crispy and flakes easily with a fork. Serve with lemon wedges.

Nutritional Information

- Total Fat: 6.8g| Saturated Fat: 1.5g| Trans Fat: 0.1g| Protein: 18g| Cholesterol: 62mg| Sodium: 267mg| Total Carbohydrates: 2.5g| Dietary Fiber: 0.8g| Sugars: 0.7g

49. Asian Fish No

Cook Time: 10 Min

What You'll Need

- 4 (4-ounce) halibut fillets
- 2 tablespoons light soy sauce
- 1/3 cup dry sherry
- 1 tablespoon brown sugar
- 3/4 teaspoon ground ginger
- 1 (6-ounce) package frozen snow peas, thawed
- 1 (15-ounce) can whole baby corn, drained

What To Do

- Coat a large skillet with cooking spray and heat over medium-high heat until hot.
- Add the fillets to the skillet and cook for 3 to 4 minutes per side, or until the fish flakes easily with a fork. Remove the fillets to a platter and cover to keep warm.
- In a small bowl, combine the soy sauce, sherry, sugar, and ginger; add to the hot skillet. Cook over high heat for 2 minutes, or until the mixture begins to thicken, stirring constantly to loosen the particles on the bottom of the skillet.
- Add the snow peas and corn, stirring until heated through. Return the fish to the skillet, turning to coat with the sauce.

- Serve the fish topped with vegetables and sauce.

Nutritional

Total Fat: 1.5g| Saturated Fat: 0.3g| Protein: 24g| Cholesterol: 56mg| Sodium: 663mg| Total Carbohydrates: 14g| Dietary Fiber: 2.3g| Sugars: 6.3g

50. Ensenada Shrimp Tostadas

Preparation Time: 25 Minutes

Ingredients

- 1 tablespoon vegetable oil
- 2 tablespoons lemon juice
- 1 teaspoon plus 1 teaspoon chili powder
- 1/2 teaspoon ground cumin

- 12 ounces medium-size cooked shrimp
- 1/3 cup fat-free sour cream
- 1/3 cup fat-free mayonnaise
- 1/4 cup fresh cilantro, chopped
- 1 can (4 ounces) diced green chilies
- 6 6-inch corn tortillas
- Nonstick cooking spray
- 3 cups shredded fresh cabbage
- 3 ripe medium tomatoes, chopped
- 3/4 cup chopped white onion

Directions

- Heat vegetable oil in skillet. In a medium bowl, pour lemon juice, 1 teaspoon chili powder, and cumin over shrimp and toss lightly. Pour into hot skillet and heat through, approximately 5 minutes.
- Prepare the dressing by mixing fat-free sour cream, fat-free mayonnaise, cilantro, chilies, and 1 teaspoon chili powder.
- Heat corn tortillas on both sides in a skillet sprayed with nonstick cooking spray.
- To prepare each tostada, place a hot corn tortilla on the serving dish. Place 1/3 cup hot shrimp mixture on tortilla. Top with 1/2 cup shredded cabbage, 1/2 chopped tomato, and 2 tablespoons chopped onion. Pour 1/4 cup dressing

over and serve immediately. Garnish with additional cilantro if desired.

Nutrition Information

- Carbohydrates: 24g| Protein: 16g| Fat: 4g| Saturated Fat: 1g| Sodium: 354mg| Fiber: 4g

CPSIA information can be obtained
at www.ICGtesting.com
Printed in the USA
LVHW050604280621
691310LV00007B/119